America's Most Important Documents

Inquiry into Historical Sources

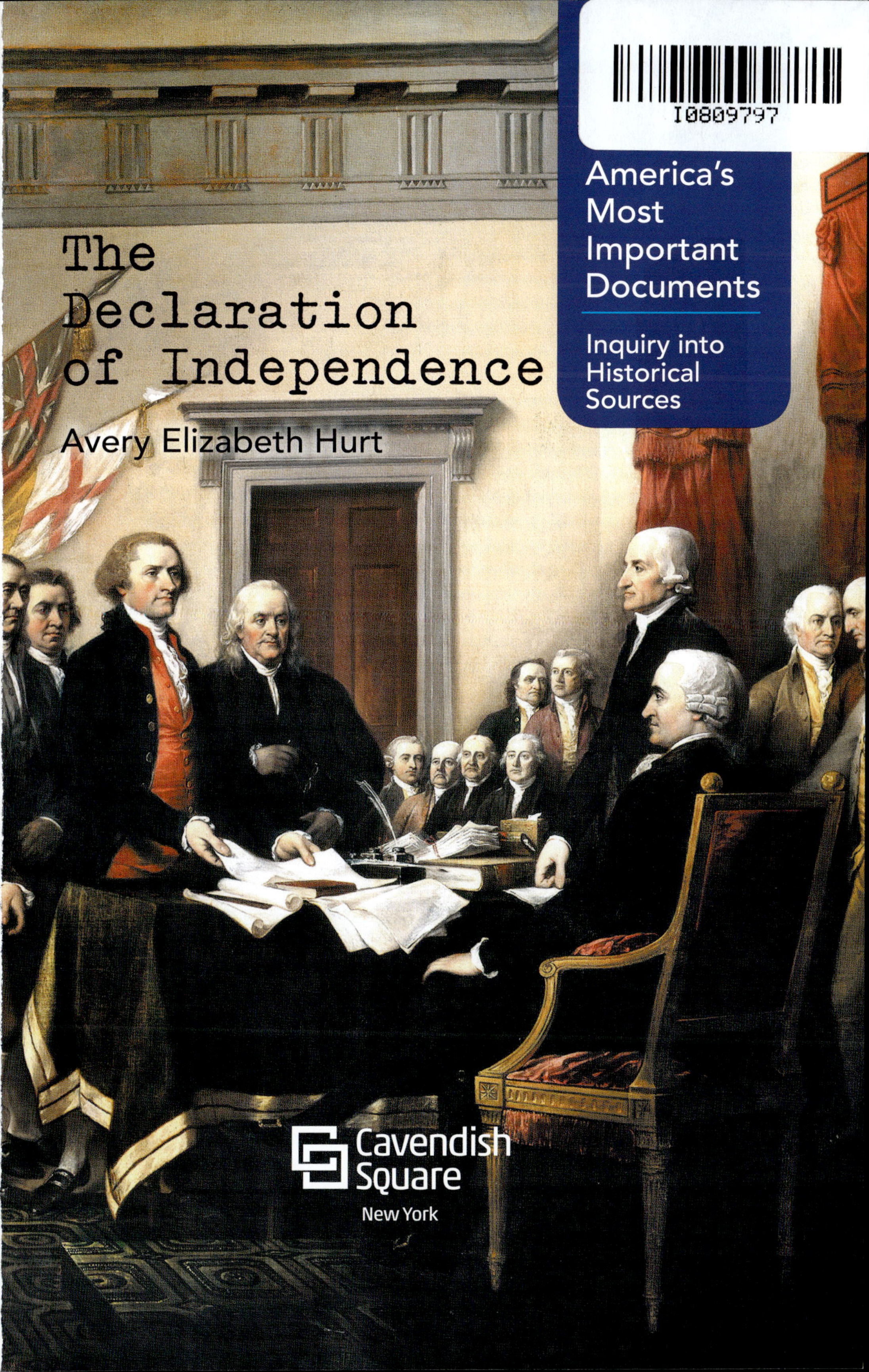

The Declaration of Independence

Avery Elizabeth Hurt

Cavendish Square
New York

Published in 2019 by Cavendish Square Publishing, LLC
243 5th Avenue, Suite 136, New York, NY 10016

First Edition

Library of Congress Cataloging-in-Publication Data

Names: Hurt, Avery Elizabeth, author.
Title: The Declaration of Independence / Avery Elizabeth Hurt.
Description: First edition. | New York : Cavendish Square, 2019. |
Series: America's most important documents: Inquiry into historical sources | Includes bibliographical references and index.
Identifiers: LCCN 2018000510 (print) | LCCN 2018001736 (ebook) | ISBN 9781502636058 (eBook) | ISBN 9781502636041 (library bound) | ISBN 9781502636065 (pbk.)
Subjects: LCSH: United States. Declaration of Independence--Juvenile literature. | United States--Politics and government--1775-1783--Juvenile literature. | United States--Politics and government--1775-1783--Study and teaching (Elementary)
Classification: LCC E221 (ebook) | LCC E221 .H87 2019 (print) | DDC973.3/13--dc23
LC record available at https://lccn.loc.gov/2018000510

Editorial Director: David McNamara
Editor: Kristen Susienka
Copy Editor: Alex Tessman
Associate Art Director: Amy Greenan
Designer: Joe Parenteau
Production Coordinator: Karol Szymczuk
Photo Research: J8 Media

The photographs in this book are used by permission and through the courtesy of: Cover Painting/Alamy Stock Photo; p. 4 Photodisc/Thinkstock; p. 7, 8 North Wind Picture Archives; p. 9 Frances Roberts/Alamy Stock Photo; p. 11 Universal History Archive/UIG/Getty Images; p. 13 Historica Graphica Collection/Heritage Images/Getty Images; p. 14 Library of Congress/Wikimedia Commons/File:Battle of bunker hill by percy moran.jpg/Public Domain; p. 17 Photo Researchers/Science History Images/Alamy Stock Photo; p. 19 Joe Griffin/Hulton Archive/Getty Images; p. 20, 40, 50 Stock Montage/Getty Images; p. 22 Universal History Archive/UIG/Getty Images; p. 24 GraphicaArtis/Getty Images; p. 28 Print Collector/Getty Images; p. 30 MPI/Getty Images; p. 31 Archivart/Alamy Stock Photo; p. 33 Everett Historical/Shutterstock.com; p. 35 Anneka/Shutterstock.com; p. 38 Charles Brutlag/Shutterstock.com; p. 42 Three Lions/Getty Images; p. 45 Epics/Getty Images; p. 46 Hulton Archive/Getty Images; p. 52 Underwood Archives/Getty Images; p. 53 Francis Miller/The LIFE Picture Collection/Getty Images.

Printed in the United States of America

Contents

1 The Slow March Toward Revolution 5

2 A Radical Announcement 21

3 Striving to Live Up to the Promise. 43

Glossary. 55

Further Information 57

Bibliography. 59

Index 62

About the Author 64

IN CONGRESS, JULY 4, 1776.
Declaration of the thirteen united States of America

Chapter One

The Slow March Toward Revolution

"We hold these truths to be self-evident ... " Every American knows the words that begin the Declaration of Independence, the document that officially separated the American colonies from Britain and began the American Revolution. However, the story of how the colonies came to feel they needed to free themselves from the British, how they justified their cause, and who the people were whose politics and philosophy stood behind the revolution is a fascinating and often surprising tale—and it began well before July 1776.

Opposite: The Declaration of Independence established the colonists' desire for freedom. It has influenced other countries for generations since.

Setting the Stage

By the time the Declaration was written, the colonies had been at war with Britain for several years. Like most wars, it is difficult to pinpoint exactly when the American Revolution began or even why it started. Tensions had gradually increased between the American colonies and the government in London. Before the tensions escalated, however, the colonies had gotten along quite well with the British—or at least they hadn't had much reason to complain. For a long time, the British government was preoccupied with matters in Europe and gave little attention to its North American colonies. However, in 1763, after the British won the French and Indian War, things changed. Britain had gained control of all of the eastern part of North America. The British Empire was the largest and richest empire since the fall of Rome. It held territory from India in the east to the Mississippi River in the American Midwest. However, as is so often the case with empires, Britain was deeply in debt and plagued by inefficiency and corruption.

Taxes, Tyranny, and Trouble

Meanwhile, the American colonies were thriving—socially, culturally, and especially economically. North America was rich in natural resources. Land was scarce in England, but there was plenty of it in North America. The colonists were able to produce most of their own food. The climate was good, and most of the land was fertile. The rivers, streams, and seas were filled with fish. Clearing the land to make room for crops provided them with plenty of wood for building houses and towns. They also used the wood to make ships. The colonists

Many people in the colonies before the revolution were quite prosperous. This image shows a wealthy Dutch family in colonial times.

traded with other countries, and many colonists became quite wealthy from importing and exporting goods.

The British Empire realized that they had a ready source of cash in the colonies. In 1765, they passed the Stamp Act. This was a tax on all forms of paper—newspapers, legal documents, pamphlets, and even playing cards. English citizens had been paying a similar tax for decades, but the colonies weren't happy about it. They petitioned the English Parliament and expressed their objections. They were ignored. Even though the tax did not amount to that much money, the colonists had a good reason for objecting: Because they were not allowed to send any representatives to Parliament, they did not get to vote on taxes that were imposed on them. No one in the colonies had a say about which taxes should be levied or what should be done with the money collected. The colonists believed that they should be taxed only by their own colonial assemblies, where colonists

The American colonists staged many protests and boycotts of English tax policy.

served as elected representatives. They campaigned against the tax using the slogan "Taxation without representation is tyranny." This emphasis on the principle rather than the practical was to be a key feature of the rationale that eventually led to the American Revolution. The people who lived in the colonies were very aware of the potential abuses of power. They did not like some of the specific things Parliament was doing. What troubled them most, however, was the arbitrary and authoritarian way they were doing it.

The colonists did not limit their objections to slogans. They organized boycotts of the taxed goods. They took to the streets to protest. A group of colonists who called themselves the Sons of Liberty began threatening and intimidating tax collectors. It worked. Soon the British repealed the Stamp Act. They did not stop trying to get revenue from the colonies, however.

In 1767, Parliament hit the colonies with yet more taxes. The Townshend Acts levied taxes on paper, glass, paint, and tea. The tax on tea was particularly irksome; the colonists drank enormous amounts of it every year. Many of them also made huge sums of money importing and selling tea. Yet here again, the cost of tea—or anything else—was not the problem. The tension between the Crown and the colonies went much deeper than that. The revenue from the Townshend Acts taxes was meant to be used to pay the salaries of the royal governors of the colonies—these were men appointed by the king to govern

The colonists loved their tea. It was also a profitable business for many colonists.

the colonies. Up to that point, their salaries had been paid by the colonial assemblies. This change was an attempt to reduce the power of the elected representatives in the colonies and increase the power of the governors, who would no longer answer to the assemblies. The colonists' complaint was about something more fundamental than paying more taxes. Using the taxes gathered from the Townshend Acts to change who the governors answered to made that problem worse.

The Situation Becomes Intolerable

The colonists carried on with boycotts and protests of the Townshend Acts, just as they had with the Stamp Act. Many even gave up drinking tea—and that was a big sacrifice. Parliament soon bowed to the pressure and repealed the Townshend Acts as well—all but one. They left the tea tax in place as a symbol of England's right to tax its colonies.

After the other taxes were repealed, the colonists stopped the boycotts of these products. Some colonists even began to drink tea again. Many, however, switched to Dutch tea that had been smuggled into the colonies. It was cheaper than legally imported tea. Drinking smuggled Dutch tea was also a way of showing the British exactly how they felt about those taxes. It likewise created financial problems for the East India Company, the primary marketer of tea in the British Empire.

In 1773, Parliament passed the Tea Act in an attempt to help the East India Company. This act gave the giant tea company permission to import tea directly to the colonies without going through England first and paying taxes there. Since the company saved money on taxes, they were able to charge less for the tea when they sold it in the colonies. This made tea cheaper in the colonies. Cheaper tea might have been welcomed, but the Tea Act irritated the colonists anyway. It basically gave the East India Company a monopoly on tea sales in the colonies, cutting out colonial merchants who previously had bought the tea at auction in London and then resold it in the colonies. However, rich colonial merchants were not the only ones rankled by this latest move. Even colonists who didn't care who could and could not sell tea were incensed by the Tea Act. To many, the law looked like a way to pacify the colonists (who did love their tea) into accepting the right of the British to impose taxes on them. To some it was just another bullying move on the part of the Crown. In any case, the colonists weren't having it.

The Sons of Liberty responded with what today we call the Boston Tea Party. On December 16, 1773, one hundred or so men disguised themselves as Native Americans and snuck aboard several ships that were docked in Boston Harbor. They dumped the cargo—342 chests of tea—directly into the harbor.

The Boston Tea Party was a protest that Britain could not ignore. This illustration imagines what the event was like.

And Furthermore

The amount of tea dumped into Boston Harbor would have made nineteen million cups of tea.

The British government hit back quick and hard with a series of laws meant to punish the colonists and recoup the money for the tea. They closed Boston Harbor until the city had paid for the tea. (This was a huge blow to the economy of Boston and the rest of the colonies.) They appointed a British general as governor of Massachusetts. They sent more troops to keep order in the city. The names of these new laws say it all. The British called them the Coercive Acts. They meant to coerce—or force—the colonies into submission. The colonists called them the Intolerable Acts.

The Fighting Begins

In September 1774, representatives (called delegates) from twelve of the thirteen colonies met in Philadelphia to discuss the situation. (Georgia did not send a delegate because the colony was in the midst of an uprising of the native tribes. They didn't want to alienate the British Army in case they needed help.) At this meeting, called the First Continental Congress, the delegates issued the Declaration of Rights and Grievances. This document basically affirmed that the colonies were loyal subjects of the British Empire. However, it clearly stated that the British Empire had no right to tax the colonies. The delegates also agreed to boycott goods from England until the Coercive/Intolerable Acts were repealed. The delegates agreed to meet again the following May. If Parliament had not come around by this time, the colonies would stop shipping goods to England. It was, at this point, largely a trade war.

John Adams, Gouverneur Morris, Alexander Hamilton, and Thomas Jefferson met together at the First Continental Congress in 1774.

While the delegates were issuing ultimatums and debating trade policy, the situation throughout the colonies was growing more serious. Shortly before the scheduled Second Continental Congress in May 1775, British soldiers attempted to seize weapons the colonists had stockpiled. The weapons were stored in the small towns of Lexington and Concord, just outside of Boston. In April, armed colonists met the British troops as they marched toward the towns. A bloody skirmish, called the Battle of Lexington and Concord, followed. The trade war turned quickly into a real war.

While the Second Continental Congress was in progress, more violence erupted. American militia members—about one thousand of them—built a series of fortifications on Breed's Hill, just outside Boston. They were attempting to prevent British troops from occupying the area. On June 17, British troops marched on the fortifications. The colonists were in place, but they had a very limited amount of ammunition and couldn't afford to waste any. As the British approached, the leader of the colonial militia, Colonel William Prescott, uttered a now-famous line. He said, "Don't fire until you see the whites of their eyes." The Americans held their fire until the British were within a few dozen yards, then let loose with a barrage of musket fire. The British retreated, reformed, and attacked again. By the third time the British attacked, the patriots were dangerously low on ammunition. This time, they fought hand-to-hand. The Americans were vastly outnumbered. Once their ammunition ran out, they were forced to retreat. The British took the hill and won the day. (A last-minute change of location—from Bunker Hill to Breed's Hill—caused this battle to go down in history as the Battle of Bunker Hill rather than the Battle of Breed's Hill.) But the victory was a Pyrrhic one. Some eight hundred

The British took heavy losses at the Battle of Bunker Hill.

British troops were killed, and hundreds more were wounded. The Americans lost one hundred people, with three hundred wounded. These were significant losses, but still not as much as the British had lost.

The Battle of Bunker Hill, though a defeat for the American militia, proved two things: the patriots meant business, and the British would not defeat them easily.

Meanwhile, back in Philadelphia, the delegates realized that a war had begun—even if it was not yet clear what they were fighting for. Were they fighting for independence from Britain? For representation in Parliament? For more respect from the British government? No one seemed to know exactly. They did know, however, that the colonists were willing to take up arms to defend their rights. The delegates created the Continental Army and put George Washington in charge of it. They justified this decision with a document called the Declaration of the Causes and Necessity of Taking Up Arms. They asked two men to write the document, John Dickinson of Pennsylvania and Thomas Jefferson of Virginia.

This declaration, as truculent as it was, did not come even close to demanding independence from Britain. Instead, it attempted to explain that Parliament had overstepped its authority with regard to the colonies, and why Britain should

And Furthermore

Many of the Founding Fathers were quite young in 1776. James Monroe was eighteen; Alexander Hamilton was probably only nineteen; James Madison was twenty-five, and Thomas Jefferson was thirty-three. King George III wasn't all that old either. He was thirty-eight.

treat the colonies with greater respect. At this point—despite bloody battles and the establishment of a continental army—the colonists weren't making a case for independence. It seems odd, but the colonists were fighting a war against Britain while simultaneously declaring their loyalty to the mother country.

Threats and Peace Offerings

In an attempt to put an end to the fighting—and perhaps to temper somewhat the tone of the latest declaration—the colonists also sent the king something known as the Olive Branch Petition. It also explained why they were taking up arms, but asked the king to help with the situation.

The Olive Branch Petition was basically a request that King George intervene with Parliament on behalf of the colonies. It began with these words: "We your Majesty's most faithful subjects of the colonies … " It went on to say that war between the colonists and the mother country was "abhorrent to the affection of your still faithful colonists … " No doubt a lot of work and diplomacy went into the careful wording of the petition.

It was all in vain though. King George refused to even read the petition, much less consider its request. This not only demonstrated to the colonists that Parliament and the king's ministers had the sovereign's full support, but it insulted the colonists as well. Until this point, the colonists had placed most of the blame for their troubles on Parliament and given the king a pass. That was the case no longer.

As we shall see, the king soon became the focus of much of the colonists' complaints and invective. The Declaration of Independence would portray him as a tyrant who had no right to rule. King George was not himself responsible for the policies so hated by the colonies, but his ministers were, and he was supportive of his government. Had he at least read the petition and made a few concessions, things might have gone very differently, because at this time, most colonists didn't want independence.

Back then, the colonists were enjoying a fairly high standard of living—higher, in fact, than their fellow citizens back home in England. As the Declaration of the Causes and Necessity of Taking Up Arms made clear, most colonists considered themselves loyal subjects of Britain. Few were interested in separation from Britain. So why were they so ready to risk life and limb fighting the Redcoats (as they called the British soldiers)? Clearly, the colonists were a feisty bunch. They had enjoyed relative autonomy for a long time. If they had been used to a lot of intervention in their polices (taxes and other matters) from the imperial government, they might not have been so upset about the Stamp Act or even the Townshend Acts (though it is hard to imagine them sitting quietly while their precious tea was taxed!). What really galled the colonists, however, was the interference from a government all the way across the ocean. They had been doing quite well managing their own affairs and hoped to keep it that way. For most colonists, the matter was more like a squabble among family members than a colonial revolution.

Thomas Paine, author of *Common Sense*

The Final Push: It's Just Common Sense

The colonists were certainly riled up and fed up with the British. But for the most part, they were not quite ready to go so far as independence. There was a mood taking shape in the colonies, but no one had really put it into words. Ideas and slogans like "taxation without representation" were specific complaints. But there was something deeper afoot. It took a recently arrived Englishman to put it into words—and push the colonists toward outright revolution.

Thomas Paine was born in England and had very little success in his native country. Once he immigrated to Philadelphia, in 1774, he found his purpose in life. While working as an editor of the *Pennsylvania Magazine*, he wrote many essays and articles on a wide range of subjects. One day a friend asked him to write a pamphlet making the case for why the colonists should separate from Britain. Paine agreed. The pamphlet he wrote became one of the most

Declaring a New Nation

However, the argument for revolution—or separation from England, as it was called then—was growing. The arrogance of the British government made the colonists even angrier. The mood in the colonies was rapidly changing from "we need more respect" to "we need to be independent." The delegates to the Continental Congress seemed to have seen the writing on the wall.

important documents in the history of the United States. It had a huge influence in other places as well. He called the work *Common Sense.* It was a good title because the pamphlet used language everyone—even people with little education—could understand. Paine wrote that all people had rights, simply because they were human. He demolished the argument for the hereditary right of kings.

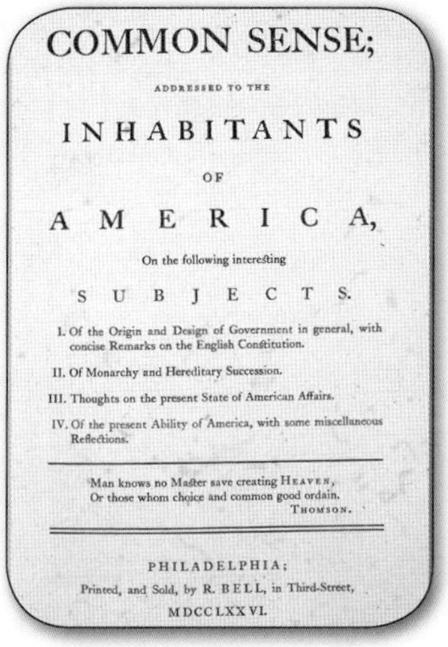

COMMON SENSE;

ADDRESSED TO THE

INHABITANTS

OF

AMERICA,

On the following interesting

SUBJECTS.

I. Of the Origin and Design of Government in general, with concise Remarks on the English Constitution.

II. Of Monarchy and Hereditary Succession.

III. Thoughts on the present State of American Affairs.

IV. Of the present Ability of America, with some miscellaneous Reflections.

Man knows no Master save creating HEAVEN,
Or those whom choice and common good ordain.
THOMSON.

PHILADELPHIA;
Printed, and Sold, by R. BELL, in Third-Street,
MDCCLXXVI.

Common Sense helped launch the American Revolution.

The response was overwhelming. Almost everyone in the colonies read *Common Sense* or heard it read aloud. It did indeed seem like good old-fashioned common sense. Thanks to Paine's pamphlet, support for independence mushroomed. *Common Sense* was a major influence on the Declaration of Independence as well.

Once the delegates realized that separation was all but inevitable, they needed another declaration. This one would have a very different tone from the previous declarations. Where those had emphasized the loyalty of the colonies to the Crown, this one would need to make a strong case against the Crown. It would need to justify the revolution. The delegates agreed that the best person for the job of writing this document was a young man from Virginia named Thomas Jefferson.

Chapter Two

A Radical Announcement

In 1776, the mood for independence was strong and growing stronger, but it was not official yet. On June 7, 1776, in the Second Continental Congress (it lasted from 1775 to 1781), a delegate from Virginia named Richard Henry Lee introduced a resolution calling for independence. By this time, most of the delegates were in favor of independence but not all. Some of the delegates were not quite ready for such a drastic move. Even some of the delegates who favored independence or thought that it was inevitable couldn't vote yet. They needed instructions (and support) from the people they represented before they could agree to the resolution.

In addition, separation from Britain posed some tricky problems for the Continental Congress. They had to justify the decision to the public, of course. They also had to convince other

Opposite: The signings of the Declaration of Independence and the Constitution took place in what is known today as Independence Hall.

European nations to recognize the colonies as an independent nation. The new republic would need allies, and persuading other nations to work with the upstart colonies and treat them like an autonomous nation (rather than British colonies) would not be easy.

So they did what governing bodies so often do when facing tough issues—they formed a committee. Actually, they formed three committees in response to Lee's resolution. One was intended to come up with a plan for creating alliances with other governments. Another was to start working out the details of how the colonies would operate as a united group. The third committee, however, is the one we remember most today. The purpose of the Committee of Five, as this one was called, was to draft a document explaining why the colonies were breaking away from England. This was meant to justify the separation to foreign nations. The document they produced did that, and so much more. It was called the Declaration of Independence, and it became one of the founding documents of the new nation. It still influences how the United States government operates and how the people of the United States think of themselves as a nation today.

Thomas Jefferson (*right*) wrote the document, but others helped him polish it.

The members of the committee were John Adams from Massachusetts, Benjamin Franklin from Pennsylvania, Roger

Livingston from New York, Roger Sherman from Connecticut, and Thomas Jefferson from Virginia. Jefferson, who was thirty-three years old at the time, was one of the youngest delegates to the convention.

A Peculiar Felicity of Expression

Despite his youth, Thomas Jefferson was exceptionally accomplished, and was already considered a first-rate thinker. He was gifted in languages. In addition to English, he spoke French, Italian, and Latin, and could read Greek and Spanish. There is some evidence that he studied German and Welsh as well. He attended the College of William and Mary in Virginia. There he studied literature, rhetoric, science, mathematics, and philosophy. After completing his studies at William and Mary, he went on to study law under George Wyeth, a well-respected legal scholar and teacher. Jefferson was admitted to the Virginia bar in 1767 (which meant that he had met the requirements to practice law in Virginia). From 1769 to 1774, he was a member of the Virginia state legislature. While serving there, he was active in groups that opposed British control of the colonies. In 1774, he wrote "A Summary View of the Rights of British America," a document explaining why the British Parliament did not have a right to rule the colonies. This document earned Jefferson a reputation for being someone who was well versed in the ideals of liberty and passionate for the cause of independence. These accomplishments certainly prepared Jefferson to do a good job writing the declaration. However, he was chosen to draft it primarily because he was an excellent writer.

This portrait shows Thomas Jefferson, the author of the Declaration of Independence and eventual president of the United States.

The other delegates knew that in order to make their case strong and convincing, they needed someone who would put it in powerful and beautiful language. Many years later, in a letter to Timothy Pickering, John Adams recalled how the decision was made: "Mr. Jefferson came into Congress, in June 1775, and brought with him a reputation for literature, science, and a happy talent of composition. Writings of his were handed about, remarkable for the peculiar felicity of expression." At the gathering in 1776, the delegates voted on who should be assigned the task of writing the document. Jefferson—with Adams's support—got the most votes, but Adams came in second. Jefferson insisted that Adams should have the honor. Adams refused. When Jefferson asked why Adams wouldn't write it, Adams replied that he, Adams, was "obnoxious, suspected, and unpopular," and Jefferson was just the opposite. Perhaps more importantly, Adams said to Jefferson, "You can write ten times better than I can." Jefferson accepted the assignment. And he certainly brought his "peculiar felicity of expression" to bear on what was undoubtedly the most important work he ever wrote.

Jefferson had just over two weeks to write the first draft, but it didn't take him nearly that long. Some accounts say he composed his first draft in just a day or two, and then spent the rest of the time polishing. He holed himself up in a rented room in Philadelphia, not far from the state house, and got to work. Jefferson loved books. At one time his personal library contained over six thousand of them. Of his many and varied pastimes, reading almost certainly topped the list. He had a tremendous background of knowledge to draw on in writing his great work. He was steeped in the literature of the Enlightenment, a philosophical movement that valued human reason and the liberty and independence of individuals.

While he worked on the declaration, Jefferson kept two documents close at his side. These were the draft of the Virginia Constitution (which he himself had written) and the Virginia Declaration of Rights, which had been written by George Mason earlier that same year. Both of these were documents that translated Enlightenment ideals into political action. Most of the ideals and principles set out in the Declaration of Independence were not new, and these two documents expounded many of them. Mason had written:

> *[A]ll men are by nature equally free and independent, and have certain inherent rights, of which, when they enter into a state of society, they cannot, by any compact, deprive or divest their posterity; namely the enjoyment of life and liberty, with the means of acquiring and possessing property, and pursuing and obtaining happiness and safety.*

These were treasured Enlightenment ideals that men like Jefferson, Mason, and others had been discussing and debating for a long time. When Jefferson penned the Declaration of Independence, he put his own rhetorical flair on these ideals, echoing Mason's words, but with his special artistry:

> *We hold these truths to be self-evident, that all men are created equal, that they are endowed by their Creator with certain unalienable Rights, that among these are Life, Liberty and the pursuit of Happiness.*

These words are a part of the preamble to the declaration. They are memorized by American schoolchildren and immigrants, and are the most well-known words in the declaration. We know these words so well—most Americans can recite them almost instinctively—that it is easy to forget their power, or how radical they were at the time, and how aspirational they are even today. However, the meat of the document is less electrifying to modern ears. It was a list of twenty-one charges against the king of England.

Repeated Injuries and Usurpations

Jefferson began this section by stating that King George III had engaged in a series of actions that were clearly intended to establish absolute rule—or tyranny, as he put it—over the states.

> *The history of the present King of Great Britain is a history of repeated injuries and usurpations, all having in direct object the establishment of an absolute tyranny over these states. To prove this, let facts be submitted to a candid world.*

The Declaration continued with a series of phrases that began "He has … ": "He has refused … he has forbidden … he has dissolved." Each one succinctly described how the king had violated the rights of the states. The list of George's sins includes his having dissolved the representative bodies in the colonies; interfered with the independence of judges by making them dependent on him for their jobs and salaries; kept standing armies in the colonies in times of peace; made the military superior to civil authorities; and many more offenses. Though the argument was specific and technical, the language Jefferson used to make that argument was powerful and moving: "He has plundered our seas, ravaged our coasts, burned our towns, and destroyed the lives of our people," Jefferson wrote. And in another place, the declaration reads:

In every stage of these oppressions we have petitioned for redress in the most humble terms: our repeated petitions have been answered only by repeated injury. A prince, whose character is thus marked by every act which may define a tyrant, is unfit to be the ruler of a free people.

This section goes on for several intense paragraphs. Then the declaration closes with the heart of the text, and what was no doubt a world-changing announcement:

[The representatives] do, in the name, and by the authority of the good people of these colonies, solemnly publish and declare, that these united colonies are, and of right ought to be free and independent states; that they are absolved from all allegiance to the British Crown, and that all political connection between them and the state of Great Britain, is and ought to be totally dissolved …

King George III of England

There it was. The declaration by one group of people that they would no longer be subject to the rule of another.

Peer Review

Jefferson brought the document back to the committee. There, the men who had been so impressed with his writing skills began to change it. (And further changes were made by members of Congress not on the committee.) Some of the changes were small and insignificant edits, such as changing the phrase "neglected utterly," to "utterly neglected," and adding a few references to God. In some cases, they tightened up the text and improved it. Other changes were far more substantial, and far more political. They removed Jefferson's passionate denouncement of the slave trade, for instance.

Jefferson was not pleased with the changes. For the rest of his life, he would show friends the two versions side by side. He always believed his original version was superior. It may have been in some ways, but in any case, the final document was a masterpiece. It has proven to be one of the most beloved and powerful pieces of writing in history.

If Jefferson wasn't happy with the final version, the other delegates were. They had the document printed and distributed throughout the colonies, where it was read aloud in public and reprinted in newspapers. At this point, the document had no title and was unsigned. Even so, it was clear that it was about to change the world.

A Very Old Idea

The Virginia Constitution and the Virginia Declaration of Rights were not the only documents Jefferson used for example and inspiration. The idea of the people having some rights to protect them from their governments goes back eight hundred years. In the year 1215, another king of England,

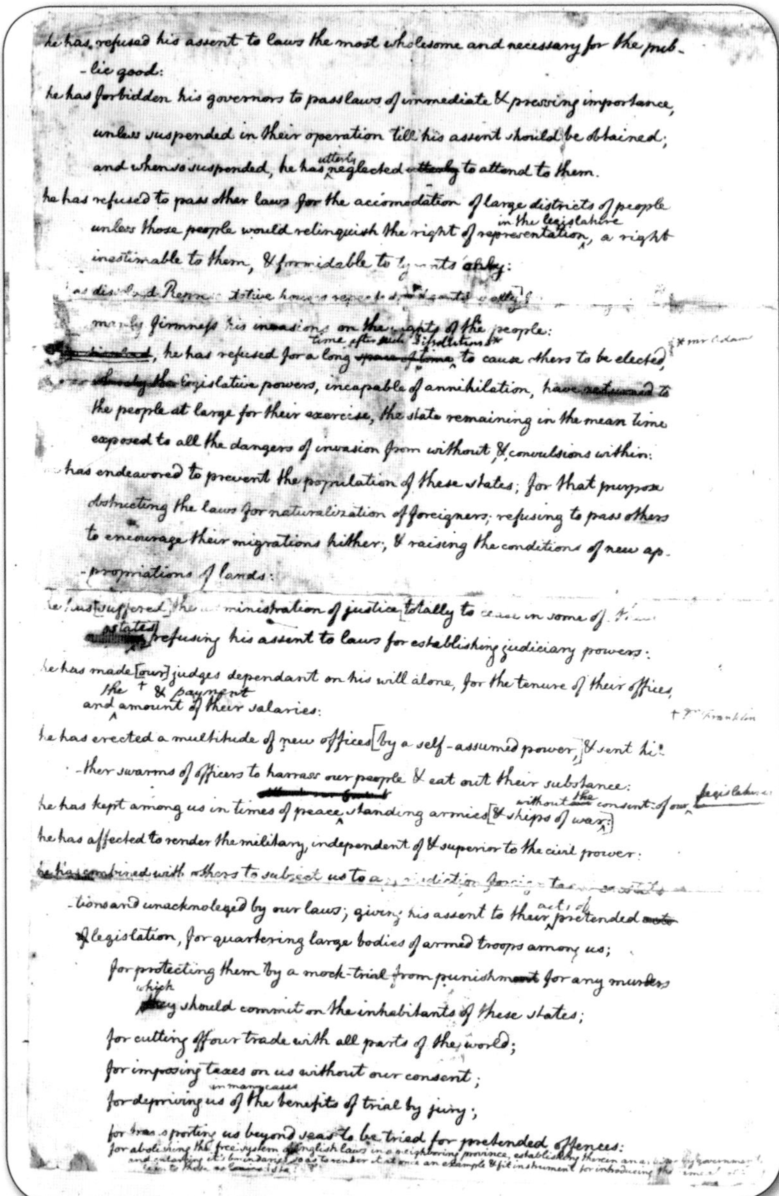

he has refused his assent to laws the most wholesome and necessary for the public good:
he has forbidden his governors to pass laws of immediate & pressing importance, unless suspended in their operation till his assent should be obtained; and when so suspended, he has utterly neglected to attend to them.
he has refused to pass other laws for the accomodation of large districts of people unless those people would relinquish the right of representation in the legislature, a right inestimable to them, & formidable to tyrants only:
he has dissolved Representative houses repeatedly & continually, for opposing with manly firmness his invasions on the rights of the people:
he has refused for a long time after such dissolutions to cause others to be elected, whereby the legislative powers, incapable of annihilation, have returned to the people at large for their exercise, the state remaining in the mean time exposed to all the dangers of invasion from without, & convulsions within:
he has endeavored to prevent the population of these states; for that purpose obstructing the laws for naturalization of foreigners; refusing to pass others to encourage their migrations hither; & raising the conditions of new appropriations of lands:
he has suffered the administration of justice totally to cease in some of these states refusing his assent to laws for establishing judiciary powers:
he has made our judges dependant on his will alone, for the tenure of their offices, and the amount & payment of their salaries:
he has erected a multitude of new offices by a self-assumed power, & sent hither swarms of officers to harrass our people & eat out their substance:
he has kept among us in times of peace standing armies & ships of war without the consent of our legislatures:
he has affected to render the military, independent of & superior to the civil power:
he has combined with others to subject us to a foreign jurisdiction, foreign to our constitutions and unacknoleged by our laws; giving his assent to their acts of pretended legislation, for quartering large bodies of armed troops among us;
for protecting them by a mock-trial from punishment for any murders which they should commit on the inhabitants of these states;
for cutting off our trade with all parts of the world;
for imposing taxes on us without our consent;
for depriving us in many cases of the benefits of trial by jury;
for transporting us beyond seas to be tried for pretended offences:
for abolishing the free system of English laws in a neighboring province, establishing therein an arbitrary government, and enlarging it's boundaries so as to render it at once an example & fit instrument for introducing the same [illegible]

Jefferson's first draft of the Declaration of Independence. Like all great writing, it had to be edited.

King John, signed a document that has a great influence on the modern world. It is called the Magna Carta (which means "the Great Charter"). In the Declaration of Independence, Thomas Jefferson described King George as a nasty, vicious, tyrant. But George had nothing on King John. John was often called "Bad King John." He was abusive and irresponsible, and eventually his nobles had enough of it.

The big problem the nobles had with John was that he had taxed them heavily to pay for foreign wars. The nobles were not interested in these wars. They did not want to pay for them. But if landholders refused to pay taxes, King John would send his army to attack their castles, seize their property, and often imprison the landowners. After a while, the nobles rebelled. They formed their own army and forced King John to sign a document agreeing that the king had to obey the law just like everyone else did.

King John of England signed the Magna Carta in 1215.

Like the US Declaration of Independence, the Magna Carta contained a long list of specific gripes the nobles had with King John. Most of these related to specific arrangements of the feudal society at the time and were no longer relevant when Jefferson wrote the declaration. But tucked away here and there in the document were some truly amazing assertions. The Magna Carta guaranteed the right to justice and a fair trial to all free men. (This was nowhere near

A Distant People Who Never Offended Him

Thomas Jefferson was a lifelong slaveholder who spent much of that life working to abolish slavery. It was one of the most perplexing contradictions in the personality of Thomas Jefferson. In the Declaration of Independence, he inserted a passage denouncing King George's support of the slave trade. Jefferson wrote that King George had "waged cruel war against human nature itself, violating its most sacred rights of life and liberty in the persons of a distant people who never offended him … carrying them into slavery in another hemisphere or to incur miserable death in their transportation thither."

Jefferson went on, in a lengthy passage, to condemn King George for resisting legislative attempts to stop the slave trade. He used language as passionate, or even more passionate, than elsewhere in the document in his tirade against the slave trade. We may never understand why Jefferson continued owning slaves, while simultaneously

everybody, of course. It has taken, and in some cases is still taking, quite a long time to extend these rights to everyone, but it was a start.) It said that the king could not put people in jail or take their belongings just because he wanted to. It said that the king could not send his soldiers to break into people's homes willy-nilly.

The most famous clause in the Magna Carta says:

This image shows the heartbreak and upset associated with being taken into slavery.

condemning the practice. However, we do know that his strong denunciation of it was removed from the declaration. Jefferson later blamed the delegates from Southern slaveholding colonies (South Carolina and Georgia) as well as Northern delegates whose fellow colonists profited from the slave trade for removing the passage. Even though the declaration had no legal weight, had the passage remained in the document, it would have been much more difficult for the colonies to continue to support slavery.

No free man shall be seized or imprisoned, or stripped of his rights or possessions, or outlawed or exiled, or deprived of his standing in any other way, nor will we proceed with force against him, or send others to do so, except by the lawful judgement of his equals or by the law of the land. To no one will we sell, to no one deny or delay right or justice.

If this sounds familiar, it is because these ideas were incorporated into the Declaration of Independence, into the US Constitution, and into US citizens' very national identity. The colonists had inherited their disdain for arbitrary authority from the very nation they were rebelling against. When combined with the Enlightenment ideal of natural rights, these limits on the reach of government were a powerful brew for inciting a revolution and forming a new nation.

And Furthermore

Thomas Jefferson and John Adams both died on July 4, 1826—exactly fifty years after the vote to adopt the Declaration of Independence.

Fifty-Five Radical Words

Though much of the declaration was devoted to criticizing King George, "the present King of Great Britain," the document actually went much deeper than that. Where the Magna Carta had focused on specific restraints on government power, the Declaration of Independence made large philosophical claims. Though the twenty-one charges against the king make up most of the text, it is the fifty-five-word preamble that is truly radical. While the rest of the document argues for a revolution against Britain, the preamble argues for a complete redesign of the relationship between citizens and their governments. It takes the ideas of the Magna Carta to a much higher level. It argues not only that the king should not be a tyrant, but that he has no right to be king, other than that given to him by the people he rules. The only power a ruler has is that power given to him or her by the people. Also, the people can revoke this at

The Declaration of Independence did not recognize the divine right of a king to rule.

any time. It argues that while there is no divine right of kings, people have natural rights.

The opening words of the declaration get right to the point. The very first paragraph begins by explaining the purpose of the document:

> *When in the Course of human events it becomes necessary for one people to dissolve the political bands which have connected them with one another ... a decent respect to the opinions of mankind requires that they should declare the causes which impel them to separation.*

This may well be the most courteous announcement of revolution that has ever been made. The declaration opens by basically saying that if we are going to rebel against you, common decency requires that we explain why.

The next words continue politely to explain that all of humanity has the right to life and freedom, and to seek happiness. Humans do not have to earn these rights. These rights are not granted by kings or governments. A person has these rights simply by being born human. However, the text continues and becomes even more revolutionary. The declaration actually claims that humans have the right—even the responsibility—to abolish governments that do not respect their natural rights. Governments, says the declaration, are given power by the people they govern—not the other way around. "That to secure these rights, Governments are instituted among Men, deriving their just powers from the consent of the governed ... " When governments deny or interfere with these rights, the people have the right to change that government or get rid of it altogether and create a new one. The declaration puts it like this: "whenever any Form of Government becomes destructive of these ends, it is the Right of the People to alter or to abolish it, and to institute new Government."

Today these ideas are so much a part of the country's national identity that it can be easy to forget just how radical they were at the time. However, this document was delivered into a world in which kings were thought to rule by the authority of God. The idea that humans actually conferred power on their governments was astonishing. Even the Magna Carta did not go that far.

Put Your John Hancock Right Here

On July 2, Congress passed Richard Henry Lee's resolution for independence. Then two days later, on July 4, 1776, they approved the revised draft of the Declaration of Independence. (The delegates from New York didn't give their approval until July 9. They had to wait for approval from their colonial assembly back home.) The draft was then printed and sent out for the public to read. Then on July 19, they made another handwritten copy for the delegates to sign. On August 2 (one month after passing the Lee resolution), they gathered for the official signing of the declaration.

The declaration had no legal weight. It was a manifesto, a pronouncement, a statement of principle. Because it was not a legal document, it did not have to be signed. Yet, after it had circulated and met with approval, the Founding Fathers did sign it. They wanted to pledge to each other their support for the aims of the document, and for the course that they had just committed themselves to. This was a very brave thing to do. Signing the Declaration of Independence amounted to an act of treason. They could be imprisoned or even executed for their involvement. At the very least, they were at risk of losing their property if this revolution did not go as they hoped. Benjamin Franklin is said to have commented, "Well,

John Hancock made sure that King George could read his signature. Today, it is one of the most well-known signatures in history.

gentlemen, we must hang together or we shall most assuredly hang separately."

John Hancock had more reasons than most of the signers for not wanting to draw undue attention to his name. He was a wealthy merchant, and made much of his money smuggling goods that had been taxed by the British into the colonies, such as glass and paper. He made a fortune smuggling Dutch tea. Though he was not among the men who dumped the cargo into the harbor, he was likely behind the Boston Tea Party. The British had more reasons than treason to go after Hancock. Yet Hancock wrote his name in big, flamboyant letters. One story says he wanted to be sure King George could read his name without having to use his spectacles. Today, people still make jokes about Hancock's bold signature. The phrase "John Hancock" has come to be slang for a signature, especially a bold, decisive one.

But no matter the size of the letters, all of the signers were bold.

Abstentions and Absentees

Not everyone signed, however. Their reasons were not fear of being hanged. Some were unable to sign because they were not in Philadelphia at the time. George Washington and Patrick Henry were among those who missed because they were absent. Some who were not available on August 2 signed at a later date. A few simply refused to sign. John Dickinson believed that it was too early to declare independence. He wanted to establish relations with allies first. He worried that the disputes between the individual colonies would lead to civil war. (He turned out to be right about that.) Also, despite his having authored the declaration justifying the use of arms, he was opposed to using violence to resolve disputes. He supported independence but hoped to achieve it without war.

And Furthermore

Eight of the men who signed the Declaration of Independence were born in England.

Another striking absence among the signers is John Jay. Jay would later be one of the authors of the Federalist Papers, a collection of essays written to support ratification of the US Constitution. These essays helped shape—and still help shape—the US government. Jay was not always an ardent supporter of independence, however. Early in the war, he had been a moderate. Like Dickinson, he was opposed to war, and believed that the colonies could work out their differences with Britain without separation. However, when England began to use military violence to enforce order in the colonies, Jay changed his mind. He was in New York that summer. Had he been in Philadelphia at the time, he probably would have signed the declaration, but no one knows for sure. A few others refused to sign because even though they agreed in principle,

Founding Father John Jay was in New York in the summer of 1776 and did not sign the declaration.

they didn't think the time was right for separation. Some who weren't in complete agreement signed anyway to help give the impression of a united Congress. In the end, fifty-six people put their names on the document, beginning one of the most significant revolutions in the history of the world.

The document that contains the words "all men are created equal" did not inaugurate a nation in which that was even remotely the case. Women were left out. So, too, were African Americans, whether slave or free. Native Americans were not included. Yet the idea was planted that all *people* were equal, that all *human beings* were equal. No one had any more right to the basics of life, liberty, and the pursuit of happiness than anyone else. And though the definition of who counts as "all men" would evolve throughout the years, the premise of equality was established. The United States is still working to live up to the promise of those words.

Chapter Three

Striving to Live Up to the Promise

After the declaration was signed, the war between the colonists and Britain became the American Revolution. It was now clear that this was a war for independence. There was no turning back. The war dragged on for another seven years. But finally it was over, and the colonies prevailed. On September 3, 1783, the United States and Britain signed the Treaty of Paris, officially ending the war. The British agreed to formally recognize the United States as an independent nation.

Too Weak to Work

Shortly after the Declaration of Independence had been signed, the Continental Congress adopted the Articles of Confederation.

Opposite: This bronze door depicts the signing of the Treaty of Paris, which ended the American Revolution.

This was the first constitution of the young United States. However, the states weren't very united by this document. It made the colonies into a very loose alliance of states and left each state with a great deal of independence. The central government was very weak, and the states were more like individual countries than one nation. The states had a lot of power to do things that is now the job of the central government, such as print currency. Paying for the war was difficult without a central currency. Technically, the Articles of Confederation placed the power of negotiating with other governments in the hands of Congress. However, Congress had no power to prevent the states from conducting foreign policy themselves. The states did. Georgia threatened war with Spain over territory in Florida. The states were already squabbling with one another, and many were busy putting down rebellions within their states. It quickly became clear that the Articles of Confederation were too weak to unite the states into a functioning government.

In 1786, Alexander Hamilton of New York suggested the new country's leaders hold a convention to discuss the problem. The other leaders agreed. The Constitutional Convention was opened in Philadelphia in May 1787. The meeting was held at what was then the Pennsylvania Statehouse. It was the same location where the Declaration of Independence had been agreed to eleven years earlier. Today it is called Independence Hall. All thirteen colonies were invited to send delegates. Twelve did. Rhode Island declined because they were opposed to a central government that would be able to interfere in the state's economy. The delegates from the other twelve colonies set to work.

Initially the aim was to address the problems with the Articles of Confederation. Soon, however, the delegates realized

Alexander Hamilton authored the great majority of the Federalist Papers.

that what was needed was an entirely new document. The Articles of Confederation created such a weak system that the country was in danger of breaking apart before it was even up and running. Drafting a constitution for the new nation was a big job. They wanted to create a government that would unify the nation and make it last for many years to come.

The details of the Constitution were much more prosaic than the poetry of the declaration. It was a blueprint for

Consequences of Signing

Most of the Founding Fathers did not suffer any ill effects from their support of the revolution, but that was not true for all. Richard Stockton, a lawyer from New Jersey, was captured and imprisoned by the British for signing the Declaration of Independence.

During the early days of the debate, Stockton had been unsure about separation from Britain. He thought that the colonists should insist on representation in Parliament. However, John Adams convinced him of the case for revolution. Stockton voted to approve the declaration and was one of the signers.

Richard Stockton, circa 1765

In the fall of 1776, the British army invaded New Jersey. Stockton rushed home. He was able to get his family to safety, but he was captured and imprisoned, under dreadful conditions. He was offered freedom in exchange for signing a loyalty oath. By this time, he was extremely ill. The king had taken over his property and his family had no means of support. Stockton signed the oath, and did not participate any more in the war effort. Later, however, he signed another oath to the state of New Jersey and the United States of America.

Nonetheless, his signature on the Declaration of Independence had cost him dearly. He lost his income and his health. He died in 1781.

operating a government, not a statement simply proclaiming the freedom and equality of all people. However, the principles and philosophy of the declaration are deeply embedded in the Constitution. The declaration was a statement of how the Founding Fathers believed things were by nature—that the rights to life, liberty, and so on were natural rights that everyone had just by virtue of being human. The Constitution was designed to create a system of government that respected and protected these rights.

Cruel Compromises

When it came down to getting the details on paper—and more importantly, getting everyone to agree—the Constitution didn't quite live up to the ideals of the declaration.

By the end of the American Revolution, several of the Northern states had either outlawed slavery or had outlawed the slave trade and were moving toward abolition. However, the Southern economy depended on slavery. Crops such as cotton, tobacco, and rice would not be profitable without slave labor. Southern landowners were not willing to give up their slaves. Twenty percent of the people in the new nation were held in indentured servitude. In the Southern states, 40 percent of the population were slaves. When the delegates began hammering out the details of the Constitution, there was a lot of controversy about how many representatives each state should have. The states with smaller populations wanted all the states to have the same number of representatives—the way it had been done in the Articles of Confederation. This would give small states a voice equal to that of more populated states. The larger states wanted the number of representatives to be based on population. But if slaves counted as a part of the population, the Southern states would come out much better. In the end, the delegates reached a compromise: The House of Representatives would have representation based on population. The Senate would be made up of two representatives from each state. There was one more detail to the compromise. In determining the population of a state, each slave would count as three-fifths of a person. The consequences of this weren't truly appreciated until much later, but this had the effect of giving the Southern states a disproportionate amount of legislative power. This was a key factor in the buildup to the Civil War in 1861.

Other compromises also made huge concessions to slave states. Congress was forbidden from banning the slave trade for twenty years, and free states were required to return runaway slaves to their owners.

These compromises were morally reprehensible, and the Founding Fathers knew it at the time. Many of the colonists and many of the Founding Fathers realized what a horrible thing slavery was. Most of them believed it should be abolished. But many of them were also slaveholders. Thomas Jefferson, the man who penned those stirring words, "all men are created equal," was himself a slaveholder. So were George Washington and George Mason (the man who wrote the Virginia Declaration of Rights). Mason said that slavery was "a slow poison" that was contaminating the "minds and morals" of the American people. Nevertheless, he remained a slave owner until he died, and did not free any of his slaves in his will. Jefferson spent a great deal of his life trying to get slavery abolished in the state of Virginia. He called slavery "a moral depravity" and a "hideous blot" on the nation. Yet he never freed a single one of his slaves, nor did he free them in his will. These contradictions were a deadly worm eating at the heart of the nation.

Many of those who opposed slavery (even many of the slaveholders) hoped that slavery would end naturally as the economy changed and the institution became obsolete. They also knew that there was no hope of ending slavery if the slave states refused to ratify the Constitution. The Northern states were willing to make these compromises with slavery because it seemed that was the only way to get the Constitution passed. Whether it was necessary or not, it was a bargain with evil. It would come back to haunt the nation. The Founding Fathers postponed until later the decision to uphold the ideal expressed in the words "all men are created equal." But those ideals did not die. It took eight decades and one of the bloodiest wars the United States has ever fought to put it right. But in the end, the words of the declaration helped bring an end to the abominable institution of slavery. In November 1863, in the midst of the Civil War, Abraham Lincoln spoke these words to people in Gettysburg, Pennsylvania: "Four score and seven years ago, our fathers brought forth on this continent, a new nation, conceived in liberty, and dedicated to the proposition that all men are created equal." Four score and seven years is eighty-seven years. Eighty-seven years

And Furthermore

Thomas Jefferson later became the third president of the United States. However, he asked that the epitaph on his tomb recognize him for only three things: that he authored the Declaration of Independence and the Virginia Statute for Religious Freedom, and that he founded the University of Virginia.

President Abraham Lincoln referred to the Declaration of Independence in his Gettysburg Address in 1863.

before Lincoln's Gettysburg address was 1776. Lincoln was not referring to the Constitution. He was referring to the Declaration of Independence. Though the nation's constitution and laws had allowed and even at times encouraged slavery, the words that had inspired a nation were still taken seriously by its citizens.

Echoes Through History

As the nation has grown and matured, it has continued to refine and extend the notion of liberty and freedom. As a result of the Civil War, amendments were added to the Constitution outlawing slavery, giving all people "equal protection of the laws," and extending the right to vote to African American men.

In the early part of the twentieth century, women echoed the Declaration of Independence as they organized and demanded the right to vote. In 1848, in Seneca Falls, New York, the women's movement began with a Declaration of Sentiments, clearly based on the Declaration of Independence. It contains these words, "We hold these truths to be self-evident: that all men and women are created equal." Women at last gained the right to vote in 1920.

And Furthermore

The Declaration of the Rights of Man and of the Citizen, the document that set off the French Revolution, was inspired by the US Declaration of Independence.

Later in that century, Dr. Martin Luther King Jr. channeled the spirit of the declaration in his famous "I Have a Dream" speech, when he called on the nation to respect the rights of African Americans. King said:

> *When the architects of our republic wrote the magnificent words of the Constitution and the Declaration of Independence, they were signing a promissory note to which every American was to fall heir. This note was a promise that all men, yes, black*

men as well as white men, would be guaranteed the unalienable rights of life, liberty, and the pursuit of happiness.

The words of the Declaration of Independence echo throughout our legal system. The declaration is quoted in at least one hundred Supreme Court opinions. Though the declaration is not law, it is very much the spirit that drives law in the United States.

The spirit of the Declaration of Independence inspired later generations of women to march for the right to vote. These women are marching in Chicago in 1920.

Civil rights leader Martin Luther King Jr. waves to the crowd during the March on Washington in 1963.

It is not only in the United States where the influence of the declaration is felt. Ho Chi Minh, the revolutionary leader of North Vietnam, was deeply influenced by Thomas Jefferson and the Declaration of Independence. He based his nation's declaration of independence from France on the US document.

The Universal Declaration of Human Rights, adopted by the United Nations in 1948, draws on some of the language and principles of the US Declaration of Independence.

Despite his rousing condemnation of the slave trade, Thomas Jefferson did not personally live up to the ideals of the document he drafted. Yet that does not mean that we cannot. The words of the declaration have echoed throughout our nation's history. They have continually reminded us of who we are, who we set out to be, and who we are capable of being. And they have held us to those values. We have not yet completely lived up to the promise of the declaration, but as long as we "hold these truths to be self-evident" we will continue to strive to reach the ideals of the Declaration of Independence.

Glossary

arbitrary Without clear reason or justification.

argument A carefully reasoned explanation for a position or opinion, often designed to convince.

autonomous Independent, self-governing.

coerce To force; to achieve using threats or intimidation.

confederation An allied group of nations or organizations.

Crown Shorthand for the ruler of a monarchy.

delegate A person acting on behalf of others at a meeting or a convention.

Enlightenment A philosophical movement that valued individual reason and autonomy over traditional authority.

felicity Accuracy or fluency in speech or writing.

feudal Regarding a medieval European class system in which peasants worked for nobles, who in turn pledged allegiance to the monarch.

imperial Having to do with or related to an empire or an emperor.

invective Strongly critical, insulting, and/or abusive language.

noble A member of European aristocracy.

olive branch A metaphor or symbol of peace, traditionally used to refer to an overture of peace.

preamble An introductory statement.

principle A basic belief or truth on which other positions are based.

Pyrrhic victory A victory that is actually a defeat because of the losses suffered in order to win (it refers to an ancient Roman battle).

radical Relating to dramatic change or a dramatic variation from tradition.

rationale The logic or reasoning behind a position, opinion, or course of action.

redress Compensation for a wrong or injustice.

rhetoric The art of persuasive speech or writing.

smuggle To bring something into a country or state illegally.

sovereign The ruler of a nation; a king or queen.

truculent Combative; ready to argue or fight.

Further Information

Books

Anderson, Marilyn. *Biographies of the American Revolution*. New York: Rosen, 2013.

Anderson, M. T. *The Astonishing Life of Octavian Nothing, Traitor to the Nation: Volume I: The Pox Party*. Somerville, MA: Candlewick, 2006.

Coddington, Andrew. *Thomas Jefferson: Architect of the Declaration of Independence*. New York: Cavendish Square, 2017.

Lowery, Zoe. *The American Revolution*. Age of Revolution. New York: Rosen, 2016.

Websites

The Jefferson Monticello

http://home.monticello.org

Operated by the Thomas Jefferson Foundation, this website contains a wealth of information about Thomas Jefferson.

Library of Congress: Declaring Independence: Drafting the Documents

https://www.loc.gov/exhibits/declara/ruffdrft.html

Read Jefferson's "rough draft" of the Declaration of Independence here.

Library of Congress: Documents

https://www.loc.gov/collections/continental-congress-and-constitutional-convention-from-1774-to-1789/articles-and-essays/timeline/1764-to-1765

Here you can find a timeline and documents from the Continental Congress and the Constitutional Convention.

National Archives: Declaration Transcript

https://www.archives.gov/founding-docs/declaration-transcript

Visit this website to view transcripts and high-resolution images of the Declaration of Independence and other founding documents.

National Archives: Founders Online

https://founders.archives.gov/

This website explores the people and writings behind the founding of the United States of America. It contains thousands of documents written by the Founding Fathers.

Bibliography

Ambrose, Stephen E. "Founding Fathers and Slaveholders," Smithsonian, November 2002. https://www.smithsonianmag.com/history/founding-fathers-and-slaveholders-72262393.

Boles, John B. *Jefferson: Architect of American Liberty*. New York: Basic Books, 2017.

Davis, Kenneth C. "The Radical Mr. Jefferson's Declaration of Independence." *Washington Post*, July 4, 1990. https://www.washingtonpost.com/archive/lifestyle/1990/07/04/the-radical-mr-jeffersons-declaration-of-independence/7a633008-f348-40e5-b79e-279562440560/?utm_term=.1a631c5186c3.

Ellis, Joseph J. *American Sphinx: The Character of Thomas Jefferson*. New York: Knopf, 1997.

Ferreiro, Larrie. "At Its Core the Declaration of Independence Was a Plea for Help from Britain's Enemies," Smithsonian, June 28, 2017. https://www.smithsonianmag.com/history/its-core-declaration-independence-was-plea-help-britains-enemies-180963857.

Hamilton, Alexander, James Madison, and John Jay. *The Federalist Papers*. New York: Bantam, 1988.

Hitchins, Christopher. *Thomas Jefferson: Author of America*. Eminent Lives. New York: HarperCollins, 2005.

Hogeland, William. *Declaration: The Nine Tumultuous Weeks When America Became Independent, May 1–July 4, 1776*. New York: Simon and Schuster, 2010.

———. *Founding Finance: How Debt, Speculation, Foreclosures, Protests, and Crackdowns Made Us a Nation*. Austin, TX: University of Texas Press, 2012.

Italie, Hillel. "What You Should Know About Forgotten Founding Father John Jay." PBSNewshour, July 4, 2015. https://www.pbs.org/newshour/nation/forgotten-founding-father.

Jefferson, Thomas, and William Peden (ed.). *Notes on the State of Virginia*. New York: Norton, 1972.

Johnson, Paul. *A History of the American People*. New York: HarperCollins, 1997.

King, Martin Luther Jr. "I Have A Dream." Speech Delivered in Washington, DC, 1963. Transcript in US Government Archives: https://www.archives.gov/files/press/exhibits/dream-speech.pdf.

Raphael, Ray. *A People's History of the American Revolution: How Common People Shaped the Fight for Independence*. New York: Perennial, 2001.

Simon, Caroline. "The Story of the Only Man Who Signed the Declaration of Independence and

Recanted His Signature." *Business Insider*, July 4, 2016. http://www.businessinsider.com/life-of-richard-stockton-2016-6.

United Nations. *Universal Declaration of Human Rights*. Illustrated Edition, 2015. http://www.un.org/en/udhrbook/pdf/udhr_booklet_en_web.pdf.

Whittaker, Harry. "Mightier than the Sword: The Impact of the Ideas of Thomas Paine on the American Revolution." *In Defense of Marxism*, March 28, 2008. https://www.marxist.com/thomas-paine-american-revolution.htm.

Wood, Gordon S. *The Idea of America: Reflections on the Birth of the United States*. New York: Penguin, 2011.

———. *The Radicalism of the American Revolution: How a Revolution Transformed a Monarchical Society into a Democratic One Unlike Any That Had Ever Existed*. New York: Knopf, 1992.

———. *Revolutionary Characters: What Made the Founders Different*. New York: Penguin, 2006.

Index

Page numbers in **boldface** are illustrations.

Adams, John, **13**, 22, 24–25, 34, 46
amendment, 51
arbitrary, 8, 34
argument, 18–19, 27
Articles of Confederation, 43–45, 47
autonomous, 17, 22

Battle of Bunker Hill, 13–15, **14**
Boston Tea Party, 11, 38
boycott, 9–10, 12

coerce, 12
Coercive Acts, 12
Committee of Five, 15, 17
Common Sense, 18–19, **19**
compromise, 47–49
confederation, 43–45, 47
Constitutional Convention, 44
Continental Congress, 12–13, 18, 21, 43
Crown, 9, 11, 19, 28
Declaration of Rights and Grievances, 12
Declaration of Sentiments, 51
Declaration of the Causes and Necessity of Taking Up Arms, 15–17
delegate, 12–13, 15, 18–19, 21, 23–25, 29, 33, 37, 44, 47–48
divine right of kings, 19, 35

edit, 29
Enlightenment, 25–26, 34

felicity, 23, 25
feudal, 31
Founding Fathers, 15, 37, 46–49
French and Indian War, 6

George III, King, 15–16, 27, **28**, 31–32, 34, 38

Hamilton, Alexander, **13**, 15, 44, **45**
Hancock, John, 38–39

imperial, 17
invective, 16

Jay, John, 39–40, **40**
Jefferson, Thomas, **13**, 15, 19, **22**, 23–27, **24**, 29, 33, 37, 44, 47–48

King, Martin Luther, Jr., 51, **53**

Lee, Richard Henry, 21–22, 37
liberty, 23, 25–26, 32, 41, 47, 49, 51–52
Lincoln, Abraham, 49–50, **50**

Magna Carta, 31–34
manifesto, 37
Mason, George, 25–26, 48

natural rights, 34–36, 47
noble, 31

offenses, 27
olive branch, 16
Olive Branch Petition, 16

Parliament, 7–10, 12, 15–16, 23, 46
politics, 5, 26, 28–29, 36
preamble, 26, 34
principle, 8, 26, 37, 40, 47, 53
Pyrrhic victory, 14

radical, 26, 34, 36
rationale, 8
redress, 28
representation, 8, 15, 18, 46, 48
revolution, 5–6, 8, 17–19, 34, 36–37, 41, 43, 46–47, 51, 53
rhetoric, 23, 26

slavery, 32–33, 47–51
smuggle, 10, 38
sovereign, 16
Stamp Act, 7, 9–10, 17
Stockton, Richard, 46, **46**

taxation, 7–12, 17–18, 31, 38
Tea Act, 10–11
Townshend Acts, 9–10, 47
treason, 37–38
truculent, 15
tyranny, 8, 16, 27–28, 31, 34

Universal Declaration of Human Rights, 53

Virginia Constitution, 25, 29
Virginia Declaration of Rights, 25, 29, 48

About the Author

Avery Elizabeth Hurt is the author of many books for children and young adults. She majored in philosophy in college, where she took many courses in political philosophy and political science. She has always been intrigued by the process that led a relatively content and prosperous colony to risk so much for the ideals of freedom and equality. She hopes that people will continue to value these principles and strive to live up to the promise of the Declaration of Independence.